THE EASY
DRAWING BOOK
FOR TEENS

the easy
DRAWING BOOK
for teens

20 Step-by-Step Projects *to* Improve Your Drawing Skills

Angela Rizza

Illustrations by Natalia Sanabria and Georgina Kreutzer

ROCKRIDGE
PRESS

Interior and Cover Designer: Stephanie Mautone
Art Producer: Meg Baggott
Editor: Alyson Penn
Illustrations © 2020 Natalia Sanabria, pp: cover, ii, vi, xii, xiii, xv, 2-5, 10-13, 20-23, 28-31, 38-41, 46-49, 56-59, 64-67, 74-77, 82-85, and © 2020 Georgina Kreutzer, pp: x, xi, xvi, 6-9, 14-17, 24-27, 32-35, 42-45, 50-53, 60-63, 68-71, 78-81, 86-89

ISBN: Print 978-1-64611-133-6 | eBook 978-1-64611-134-3
R0

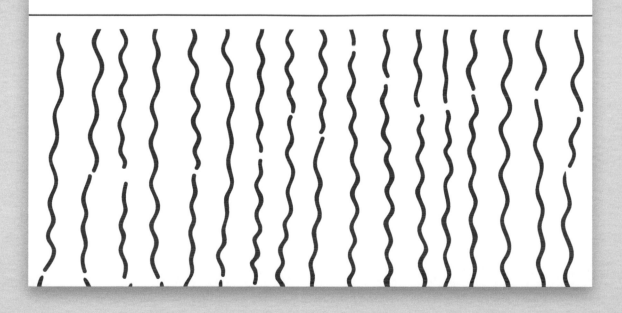

Dedicated to my mom and dad, who kept motivating me to draw and surrounded me and my art with so much positivity and pride.

Contents

Introduction

As I write this now, I can't help but reflect upon my own artistic journey, growing up dreaming of becoming a famous painter or artist just like my grandparents. Every holiday and birthday, at least one relative would give me some drawing supplies or a "how-to" book for whatever subject I was obsessed with at the time. One year, it was anime; the next, dragons; which then slipped into a long decade of bird obsession. I would spend my summers with my grandparents, where they would teach me oil painting and how to look at life and re-create what I saw. Then during the school year, I'd fill up my course load with all the art classes my high school offered, sometimes taking them twice—and usually skipping lunch to get in as many as I could. I enrolled in everything from basic drawing and painting to art history, photography, ceramics, even arts and crafts, just to try everything.

Maybe some of you reading this book can relate to the constant desire to just *do* art and absorb knowledge of techniques. Or, maybe you're curious about it and have some background but would like to know more. With this book, I want to share the passion I have for learning and creating with you; this book is something I wish I had when I was a teenager. I received many books with the same old still life or fruit bowl that had such a stuffy air of classic academic learning. To me, they lacked the reality and humanity of life. I'm filling this book with the things I love, find beautiful, and think others would enjoy—with people who don't look like perfect classical sculptures you find in a museum, or generic arrangements of wooden shapes. I hope I've piqued your interest and you'll continue reading on!

I'm a visual learner, so I'm carrying that into this book with step-by-step instruction, breaking down the overall creative process and explaining how to tackle a drawing from start to finish. We review the basics before moving on to more in-depth techniques. You'll create intricate, realistic drawings in both color and black-and-white; I explain why I add specific aspects, so you can start to think in the same creative way. Throughout the book, I also include some tips you can apply to the lesson or genre of the chapter, and there is room in the book to try out your new skills before using them with your own drawings. Creativity prompts at the end of each chapter are meant to spark your imagination and inspire further progress in your skills.

I hope this book motivates you to continue learning new ways to advance in creating art, and brings you fun and satisfaction in doing so.

How to Use This Book

Approaching a new subject or trying a style outside your comfort zone can be very intimidating or overwhelming. I imagine if someone dropped down a massive 12-piece still life and said to draw it, anyone would freak out. In this book, besides breaking drawings down into steps, I also explain the artistic process to approaching any new piece and help set you up in a way of thinking that will give you a blueprint for confidently tackling any project you're given.

I want this to be more than just a copy-what-I-do book; I want to help change your thought process and give you a formula you can apply to every piece you do, starting with imagining subjects as basic shapes when you first do your light sketch. For these steps, especially in Still Life and Realistic Portraits and Figures, it could be helpful to flip to step 8 before we begin step 1. That way, you can get a better sense for the final outcome. After you sketch the basic shapes, you will start to lightly add the mid-tones, then the darker values, and finally, the details. By just looking at subjects as shapes and shadows, they become simpler to draw, and focusing on accurately re-creating them can step up your drawing game. At the end, when you add those final fun details, they bring everything together.

Along with four activities in each chapter, I also include smaller practice workouts such as Key Detail Practice and Technique Study that can serve as warm-ups for more complicated steps. For those warm-ups, feel free to doodle in your sketchbook or grab a scrap piece of paper. Each exercise is done in grayscale pencil, until the final chapter's exercise, which is in color. If you loved one of the grayscale pieces you created, feel free to repeat that exercise in color for a bonus challenge!

TOOLS

I didn't want this book to be too complex or for you to go nuts spending money on a whole variety of art supplies. I want these exercises to be accessible to everyone, so you can start them as soon as you turn to the first page. The tools of this book are things most people have in their house: a sketchbook or paper, some cardstock paper, tape, a ruler, scissors, some grayscale pencils, and some colored pencils. A few other helpful tools are tracing paper, a pencil sharpener and an eraser, and a nice mechanical pencil with leads of different grades.

A classic HB or #2 pencil will do, but if you can find a 2H, it will help you shade lightly if you're very heavy handed. Also, a 2B or 4B helps you get darker shadows, and they're better for blending. You can often find these pencils in sets. For paper, I'd suggest using paper meant for drawing or sketching, and avoid computer or printer paper—it tends to be thin and very slick, so it's easy to smudge your drawing with your hand. The lack of tooth, or texture, in that type of paper makes it harder to get varied strokes or shading. Also, pick up a white gel pen or paint marker to add highlights.

BASICS OVERVIEW

So now, a brief refresher on the foundational lessons of drawing. I'm sure you are aware of these terms and concepts, but it never hurts to get back to the basics.

Maybe you've heard of "left brain" and "right brain" thinking and how the left brain is more structural or analytical and it helps us with language and logic, whereas the right brain is more creative and intuitive. But what exactly does that mean? Well, our right brain is where we identify shapes and edges; recognize space, proportions, and angles; and judge the values of light and shadow. And it's there that we break down a subject and see how it's made. In a way, that is all art is—understanding the structure of something and trying to re-create it in our own visual language. Your visual language could be photo-realism or it could be decorative and folksy—it's what separates our work from another's work.

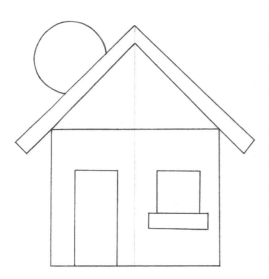

Using Guidelines— Shapes and Lines

When first looking at something, break it down into readable shapes to help simplify it. Think back to your early crayon drawings of a house that was just a triangle on top of a square with a big circle above it for the sun. Well, surprise! As an adult I still do this. Only after I throw down those shapes do I then get more advanced and add shapes within those shapes. Instead of a square window, I do a square with a half circle on top, and within that, I add a few rows of square glass panes and decorate the design with borders for a frame and add texture for the wood grain. Shapes are the start of our formula, the seeds for what eventually sprouts into a masterpiece. Identifying the different shapes in everyday objects helps change your perception of the world around you; you become more of a right-brained thinker and it gives you the essential equipment you need as an artist.

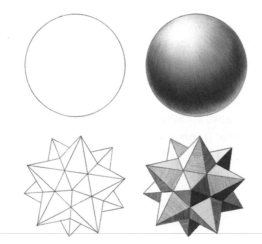

Dimension, Form, and Basic Shading

While shapes give us structure, value gives us form and dimension in our art. Observing how light interacts across a surface shows the viewer the form of something while conveying a clue as to what the subject is made of, or its texture. Line drawings are beautiful but can fall flat; shading your piece by following the contours of the lines and shapes with a variety of shades ranging from dark black to bright white can bring life to whatever you're drawing. You can do this smoothly by blending or smudging your pencil marks, or you can roughly stroke it in to represent a texture like fur, or try stylized techniques like crosshatching and stippling if you're using ink that isn't blendable.

Proportion and Scale

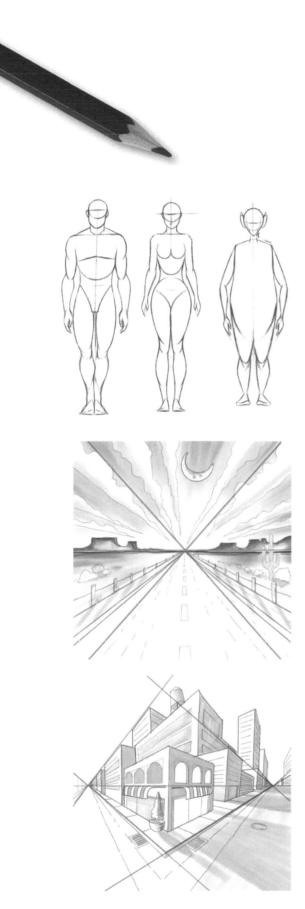

Being able to identify differences in sizes and how they relate or contrast with a subject is crucial to becoming a realistic artist. When drawing the figure, you don't just jump in and draw the whole body; you make note of where the hands fall in relation to the hip, or if the torso is longer than the legs, and how large the head is compared to their shoulders. You could be an excellent renderer and draw realistically, but if the proportions are wrong, most viewers will get the sense that something doesn't feel right, especially in portraits. It's a technical skill, and you definitely have to be a little extra observant when you take note of how everything relates in terms of scale in a piece, but not spending the extra few minutes to do that can set you up for a doomed piece before you even start.

One- and Two-Point Perspective

While value adds form to a subject, perspective adds it to your overall scene. Using lines, we create a horizon and add a vanishing point to where all lines in your scene would end. From here, we could lay out a grid, almost like a chess board, and place objects on these squares. The objects closer to us are larger, while those farther away are smaller. If you're drawing closer objects, such as those on a table, you'd notice the change of angles and line direction of the table's edges. Perspective is one more aspect of creating a convincing reality that follows the world we live in.

NEXT-LEVEL SKILLS

Now, let's touch on some skills that are broader and more unique from person to person. We all have our own idea of aesthetics, and everyone approaches art differently. Some would approach a landscape and color what they see, while others might choose to use all one color or use an interesting color combo. If I have a still life in front of me, I might crop some of the scene and focus on one part of it, while another person might zoom out and show it all, including the room it's set in. Maybe you love seamlessly blending everything together smoothly, while your friend loves to create visible markings and strokes and shading in rough textures. Here's a list of skills to add to your visual language.

Composition

The arrangement of your subjects is your composition. You can make it very symmetrical, where you divide the piece in half and lay subjects and similar shapes on either side like a reflection. Or you could make it asymmetric, where maybe all of your subjects are packed to the right with one single subject along the left side of the center. You can also arrange your compositions to follow the shape of a letter or another shape like a triangle. How you choose to lay out your piece creates a narrative that helps tell a story or evoke a feeling in the viewer. It's also a way of organizing your subjects into something harmonious.

Highlights and Master Blending

So, let's think beyond lights and darks. Imagine a gray-scale slider bar with dozens of possible shades. In life, many values around us would fall somewhere in the middle (depending on time of day), with a few areas being pushed toward that dark end where no light is, and other areas catching small amounts of pure white from your light source. Picking up on all these subtle shades and their transitions into each other will help you create a more seamlessly rendered piece that isn't so harshly contrasting.

Fine Details

Once we get past the basic shapes and values, we need some details to give our viewers information about what they're looking at. Maybe it's a painted vase or a soft, furry kitten. Toward the end of our formula, we use varied lines and strokes to re-create the textures, patterns, and fine lines that bring character and fun to our pieces. It's what makes our art become a finished piece rather than a sketch or study.

Value and Color Layering

The eye tends to gravitate more toward colorful pieces than those in black and white, but to learn the basics, you really need to focus on mastering those fundamentals first. Once you get into color, it could be harder to separate the value from the shade. A blue flower might seem darker than a red, but if you took a photo of it on your phone and desaturated it, the value of that red flower might be closer to dark gray, while the blue might lean more toward a middle-to-light gray. A number of mediums make it easy to start out with a grayscale rendering and then allow you to layer color on through a transparent medium (like oil and acrylic) or through colorized layers digitally. Colored pencils can be a bit trickier. You can start with a lightly drawn gray sketch, then lightly layer colored pencil over it, gradually building it up. This technique helps subdue some of the vivid chroma of the pencil to keep it from being oversaturated or cartoonish; it also helps you think of the values first.

ARTIST'S ADVICE

Before we head into exercises, here are some habits I incorporated into my own daily routine that helped me grow as an artist.

1. Set a schedule to do work every day; it's great discipline and gives you structure.

2. Surround yourself with things that inspire you, from books to movies to décor.

3. Have a sketchbook and draw every day, even if it's just a doodle or an idea for a piece.

4. Draw things that make you uncomfortable. You need to draw new things in new ways to grow as an artist.

5. Study anatomy—understanding what's underneath the skin helps with proportions.

6. Gather references and save them in files or buy books with great photos.

7. Have a designated workspace with good natural light, a lamp, and a comfy chair.

8. Look at art all the time. See what works and what doesn't. Apply these observations to your own work.

9. Don't try to re-create someone else's art or style. That's their voice and it's what comes naturally to them—you'll need to find your own.

10. Seriously, draw every day, and keep feeling passionate and hungry—it should be fun, not work.

CHAPTER ONE

Still Life

I still get flashbacks to weeks of having to draw the same wooden cubes and glass bottles in art class and being bored and feeling dead inside. There is a reason these objects keep reoccurring, but maybe your teacher never explained *why* we are all condemned to doing this at least a dozen times. Glass is transparent, catches and reflects light differently, and gives you a nice variety of interesting streaks of color and light traveling through it and being reflected on objects around it. Basic shapes are, well, basic. It's easy to identify the edges and see how value travels across their surfaces. If you look at a ball lit evenly, you can see it has one spot that is a bright, highlighted dot, and from there, the value gradually transitions from mid-tone to dark with a curved shadow. But I think you are old enough to move beyond these basics and choose some more fun subject matter and play with their compositions to make things more dynamic.

Before we jump into these exercises, observe a reference photo. Look at the basic shape each object is and the shapes of the areas around them. Start your sketch this way; then we'll go to value, then the details.

MORNING LATTE

 1 Begin by taking a moment to think about the scene: a coffee mug on top of a saucer. There should be some sweet treats like cookies next to it. Break down the subject's structure into basic shapes like circles and squares, and lightly sketch. Feel free to erase until you get the pose and scale right; that's why we just start with basic nondetailed shapes that take a second to draw and erase.

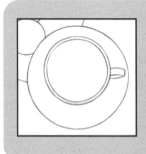

KEY-DETAIL PRACTICE
Sketch an overview of a cup in a saucer, using just circles. Warp the circles to show perspective.

2 Now, develop your simple shapes and lightly draw the outlines of the objects in the scene.

 Lightly begin shading from the darkest area of your scene to the middle tones. With this light shading, don't use much pressure; we are going to gradually build it up over time.

 Go back and begin darkening your darker shadows with slightly more pressure. Have your strokes follow the shape of the structure's form instead of following any direction.

CONTINUED ▶

MORING LATTE CONTINUED

 Start to build up your shadows with more layers and pressure. Work from the darkest edge, gradually using less and less pressure until your value matches the mid-tone values you've come to.

6 Blend out from the mid-tones to lighter values, leaving only paper where we have the highlights. Use very delicate pressure or just smudge.

Artist Trick

To avoid smudging, pull your sleeve over your hand or place a small piece of paper beneath your hand.

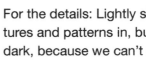 For the details: Lightly sketch your textures and patterns in, but don't go too dark, because we can't really erase this without ruining the shading.

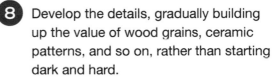 Develop the details, gradually building up the value of wood grains, ceramic patterns, and so on, rather than starting dark and hard.

GLASS ARRANGEMENT

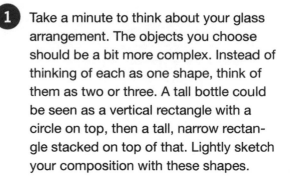

1 Take a minute to think about your glass arrangement. The objects you choose should be a bit more complex. Instead of thinking of each as one shape, think of them as two or three. A tall bottle could be seen as a vertical rectangle with a circle on top, then a tall, narrow rectangle stacked on top of that. Lightly sketch your composition with these shapes.

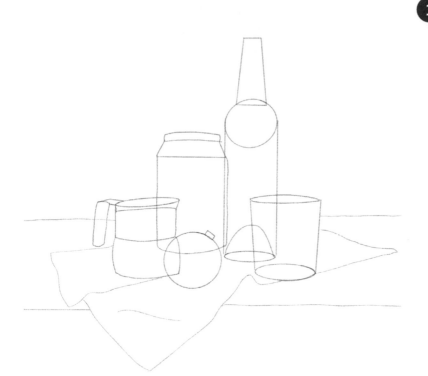

2 Continue to include more structural details. Also check the shape of the values within the bottles and reflecting on the metal. You can include these swirls and curves in your sketch to indicate the direction of your values.

Work from the darkest area to mid-tones, lightly adding shadow at first. Go back into the darker areas, adding more pressure to build up shadow.

KEY-DETAIL PRACTICE

Focus on an area of glass that reflects something behind it; delicately render the glass material and draw the warped object behind it. *Render* is an advanced word used for adding value or shading a piece.

 Darken areas where objects meet the surface. Also, on metal objects you might see some darker areas near highlights.

TECHNIQUE STUDY

Metals have harsher contrasts; their darkest value and highlight are almost on top of each other. You may have to jump from highlight to almost black immediately, then gently blend that black out to a nice mid-tone.

CONTINUED ▶

GLASS ARRANGEMENT CONTINUED

 Once darker values and mid-tones are down, lightly render out from the mid-tones with your light gray until you reach a highlight area.

 Begin indicating the details with a light sketch. Add any textural designs now.

7 Gradually build up value. For patterns it's okay to just draw lines, but for things that have form, build up and blend them into the structure's base value—don't just indicate them with dark lines.

8 Add textures and details that can be made just with short strokes. After looking at the overall piece, if some spots could pop a bit more, add a few darker shades to them.

DAILY DÉCOR STILL LIFE

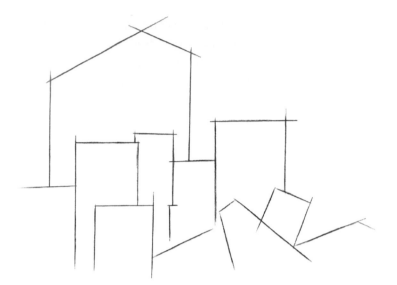

1 Basic shapes are important to start with—note them and the overall scale of everything. Arrange interesting objects in your room, such as succulents and candles, next to each other for this drawing. How does each object's size relate to objects surrounding it?

2 Sketch your composition using basic shapes, feeling free to let things overlap.

3 Begin sketching each object within your shapes, observing edges and curves. In this example, note how the bottom of the plant pot's curve almost reflects the same shape of the top curve. Think of leaves or flower petals just as simple tear shapes right now; we can define them more with some crinkling edges. Sketch out any reflective or strong shadowy curves you see.

4 Start by lightly adding value to the objects. The background can be done last; it isn't the focal point and doesn't need as much detail. Start from the center of the paper and work your way out.

TECHNIQUE STUDY

Work on shading in your sketchbook. With an H pencil, create a long rectangle and start with white, gradually building up pressure, switching to a #2 toward the middle. Then try a B pencil for the darkest end until you hit black.

CONTINUED ▶

 5 Work from the shadows, gradually building up value. Ignore minor forms like the grooves in a vase or vein creases in leaves.

6 Begin rendering the darker values, gradually building up shade. Things like leaves have multiple creases that catch the light at different angles. I like to lightly sketch where that dark-to-light transition starts, then lightly render out to match the value.

Artist Trick

For blending, try using your fingers, cotton swabs, tissue, or things around the house. Experiment and see what works best.

7 Finish rendering the object, starting at the mid-tone values and lightly blending outward toward the highlights. In the background, go ahead and add a fun wallpaper.

8 Quickly indicate the details of the rest of the scene. Add the values of the table, wall, and the shadows the objects cast. Finish the details. Add a few dark lines to indicate leaf veins, the patterns of the objects, and so on. Use short dashes to replicate wood grain.

 **KEY-DETAIL PRACTICE** If leaf veins are light-colored, leave them unshaded or use a white marker to draw them. If dark colored, start with a dark line, then blend out to soften.

COLORFUL COLLECTION

1 Focus on color for this arrangement. Pick out everyday objects—such as string lights, shoes, and sunglasses—and place them near each other. Lightly sketch the basic shapes that make up each object. Notice the angles of the surface they rest on. Using perspective lines, re-create their proper angles.

2 Develop shapes by lightly sketching out each object. Create a line drawing of everything and take note of proper scale and proportion. Sketch shadow shades, too.

3 Using colored pencils, shade shadows out with a light, neutral color like a brown or dusty blue. Avoid black.

Artist Trick

Colored pencils can be waxy, and applying too much pressure or too many layers can make it hard to add more. Start light and don't overdo your shadow color.

4 Color over the shadows with the object's main color, making little swirls to blend, along with more pressure.

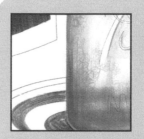

KEY-DETAIL PRACTICE

Blend complementary colors into one another. Have red transition to green, yellow to purple, and orange to blue. Take note of what works—do you need a lot of pressure, or does using many light layers work?

CONTINUED ▶

COLORFUL COLLECTION CONTINUED

5 Render lighter areas, using the main color of the object. Start from the shadow, and use a bit more pressure to make colors appear over the cooler neutral tones. Then, as you reach the mid-tones, use less pressure in the lighter areas.

6 Color the areas of scenery around them, like the wall. Start with a neutral or cool color, then layer the color on top.

 Draw the details like the line art on surfaces and patterns.

 Take a step back and just observe the overall piece. Does it need any more contrast or details? If so, add them now.

TECHNIQUE STUDY

You can go back in and begin building up with more color, slowly blending everything together. If a color is too vivid, go over it lightly with something neutral like a mid-tone brown.

FREE-FORM ART

Make your own still life filled with three to five objects you love or feel represent your personality. How can your composition or their arrangement tell a story?

CHAPTER TWO

Optical Illusions

We observe the world around us with our eyes, then re-create it through art. Let's now shift to drawing from imagination. There are different varieties of optical illusions.

Ambiguous illusion is a drawing that is a recognizable subject, but viewers may perceive it differently, like a Rorschach inkblot.

Paradox illusion can be seen in a Penrose triangle or M. C. Escher's staircase image; he plays with perspective and creates what looks like a series of stairs going down, but it is really a repeating loop.

Psychological illusion is manipulated lines, colors, and perspectives that basically override the brain and confuse it, such as geometric designs where you can see spirals and checkered patterns that vary in angle and scale and seem to move.

Cognitive illusion plays with the positive and negative space and relations of an object to show two different images. One minute you'll see a chalice, but if you look at the area around it, you can see two faces in profile.

Physical illusion or *atmospheric perspective* is when we look at a landscape and the areas closest to us are more vivid and clear, but farther away, they're duller and bluer.

For more information or inspiration, check out some of these artists: M. C. Escher, William Hill, and Salvador Dalí are very well known. Oscar Reutersvärd created the Penrose triangle along with other geometric illusions. Victor Vasarely's work was geometric and played with the unconscious. István Orosz combined mathematics and art to show and even explain optical art.

THE PENROSE TRIANGLE

 For a Penrose triangle, draw a basic triangle with three equal sides. If you have a ruler, use it for each step.

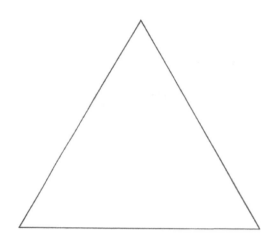

KEY-DETAIL PRACTICE
Using a ruler, first draw a mini Penrose outline to become familiar with the formula.

 From each edge tip, continue the triangle's lines just a little bit farther, having them all angling in the same direction, for example, to the left.

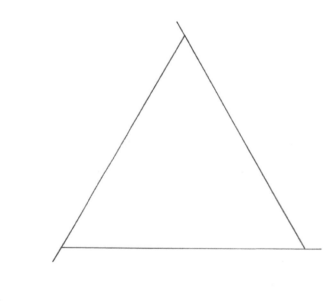

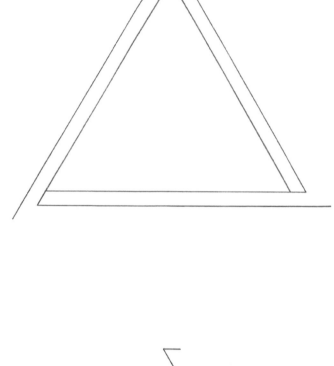

 From this extended tip, attach a line parallel to the adjacent side's line.

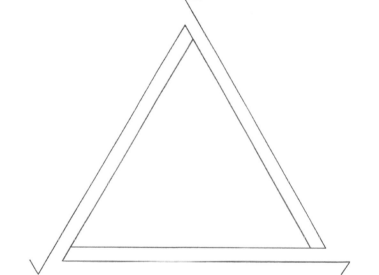

 From that new line, make a small check-mark edge.

CONTINUED ▸

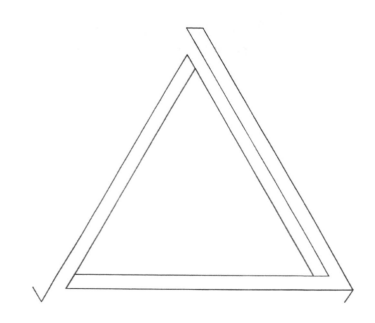

5 From that check mark, and again parallel to the side line, make sure the gaps between each triangle are equally spaced around all edges.

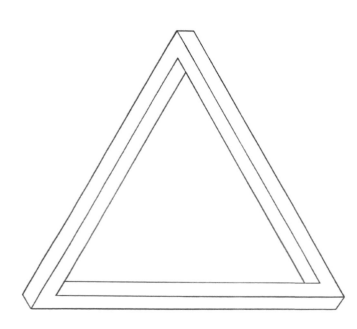

6 Connect any open gaps or corners.

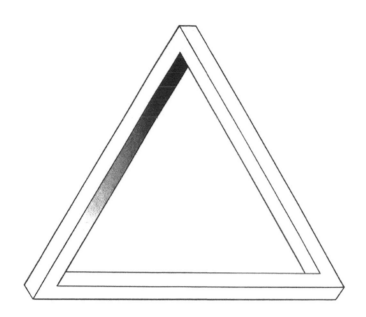

 The inner structure gets the value gradient. You'll shade from dark to light, and you should have three inner edges. At the top of the inner edge, start with your darkest value and gradually lighten up as you reach halfway down this track.

 Repeat for the remaining two corners.

Artist Trick

Plan your shading out ahead of time to prevent two mid-tones or two darks from being adjacent to each other.

OX OR ELEPHANT?

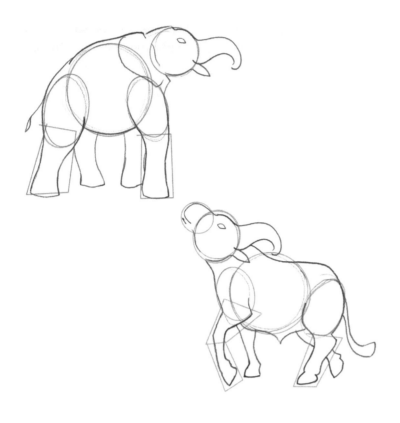

For this activity, use two sheets of tracing paper or regular paper held against a bright window.

1 On a scrap piece of paper, sketch a drawing of an ox and of an elephant so that their heads are similar in size to each other. Keep practicing until their proportions are aligned.

2 Draw the two animals on separate sheets of tracing paper, keeping in mind that their head areas should be similar shapes. Then overlap the two pages, unifying a common area like the horn or tusk.

Artist Trick

Not sure where to start? Pick two images of the same size. Using tracing paper, trace the basics of each. Overlap and rotate your two tracings, looking for where common shapes merge.

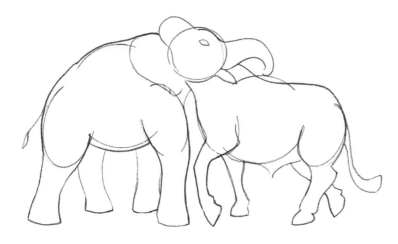

 Tape these pages to a sunny window or a light box. Place your drawing paper on top and lightly sketch the layered drawings.

 Once transferred, begin to manipulate the sketch: Erase some parts, define others. Keep going back and forth between drawing the subjects.

CONTINUED ▶

 With your sketch done, add value to complement both of your subjects. Areas under the chin and under the tail are commonly dark areas. Start to lightly sketch where shadows will go.

 Once you've established the value, begin building up shadow by using more pressure with your pencil.

7 Now add some detail lines indicating the animal's fur, anatomy, and pattern. Don't be too detailed or specific, because then the viewer will be able to easily recognize what one animal is. You want to just indicate hints of features.

8 Ask someone if they know what it is. If they answer immediately, you'll need to adjust the details so they're more ambiguous. Once you are satisfied with the results, sketch in a background image.

KEY-DETAIL PRACTICE
Focus on the eyes with this piece. We humans usually recognize the eyes first as the most identifiable, plus they're so fun to render. Sketch to tone down the eye, so we can see it as an eye and as something else, like an animal's spot pattern.

INFINITE STAIRCASE

 Start by drawing the bottom half of a 3D rectangle. Then draw equally spaced descending 90-degree stair shapes between the two vertical lines.

 Add the steps including perspective, ensuring equal space. Note you'll only see the underside of the steps.

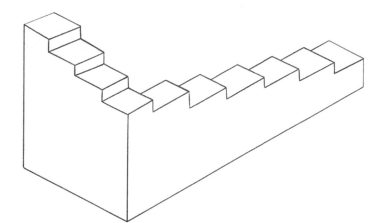

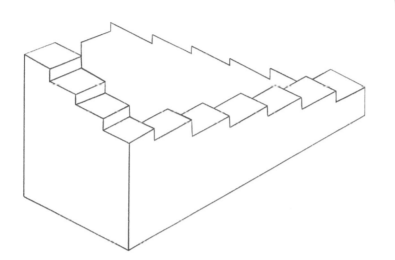

 Lightly sketch the interior edge of the two other sides of stairs to close the loop. These will be more squished and jagged 90-degree angled squares.

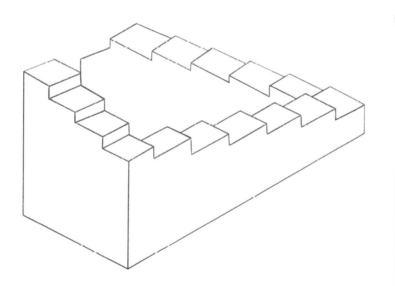

4 Draw each individual step of one side. Notice how we don't see the underside of those steps because of perspective.

TECHNIQUE STUDY

If your repeating loop is on top of a building, you'll need a convincing perspective for your architecture; create a simple one-point perspective drawing or a rectangular building.

CONTINUED ▸

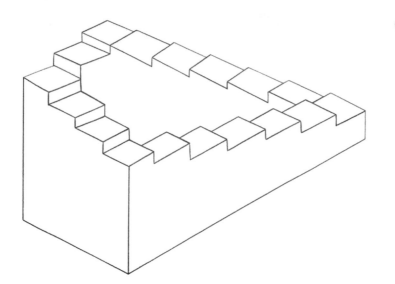

 5 The final row of stairs meets up with the 90-degree-angle side of the rectangle. Draw a step or two coming out from that interior stair edge. Put these in perspective.

6 Lightly shade. Most steps are in the light, while the walls have shadow.

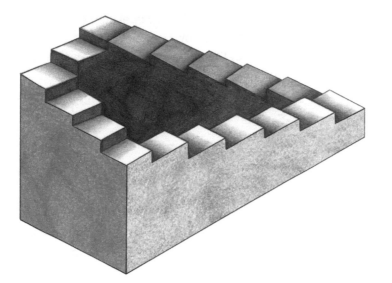

 Decorate the walls with some fun windows, vines, or flowers crawling up the sides. Are the stairs made out of wood or brick? Is someone walking on them?

 Finish the piece by adding in value and some details.

KEY-DETAIL PRACTICE
Re-create the brick texture, but sketch the stones lightly, then render with shadow.

TESSELLATIONS

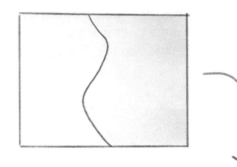

For this exercise you need cardstock paper, scissors, and tape. Cut your card into a rectangle about 3 inches by 4 inches for ease.

1 Cut a wavy line vertically down the card. Then flip the piece on the right and tape the two flat edges together.

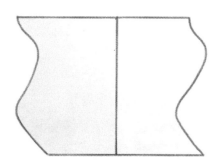

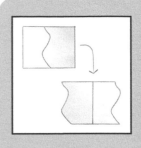

KEY-DETAIL PRACTICE

Sketch a few different tessellation designs first to see which shapes work and which don't.

2 Cut a horizontal wavy or shaped line. Flip the lower piece to the left, then tape the two flat edges together.

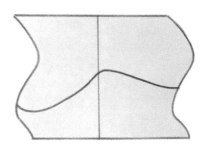

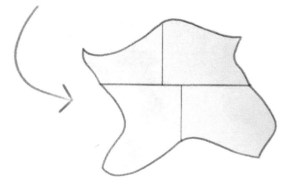

TECHNIQUE STUDY

Look at positive and negative space to get tessellations to align correctly. If there is a curve on one side, there should be an indent in the other in the exact same spot. (Think of it like fitting together pieces of a puzzle.) If there's not, you'll need to flip around your stencil.

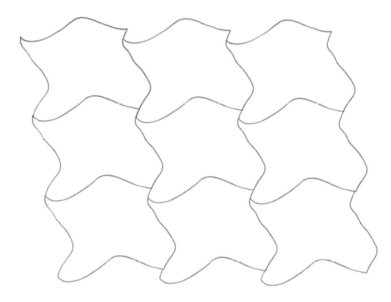

 Begin tracing your template in your sketchbook, starting at the top left of your page and continue throughout the page.

4 Go into each and lightly sketch dragon features.

CONTINUED ▶

TESSELLATIONS CONTINUED

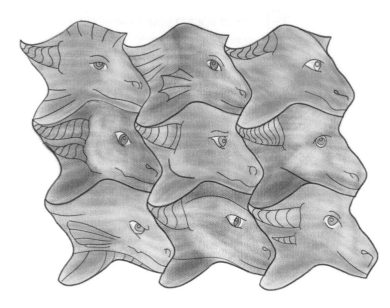

 Add color with colored pencils. To separate the puzzle, try to interchange color schemes to switch the colors in the opposite design.

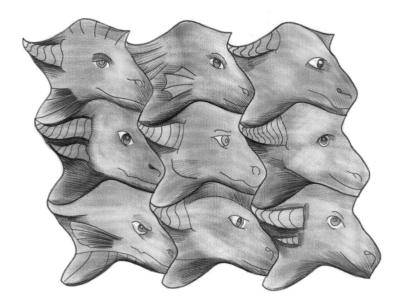

 Add some value and shadows. You can use a neutral, darker shade of brown or a cool complementary color. Continue gradually building up shadow.

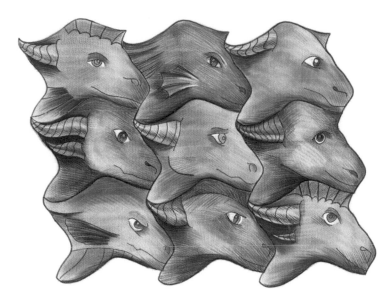

 Shade the shadows into mid-tones, then lightly render toward highlights.

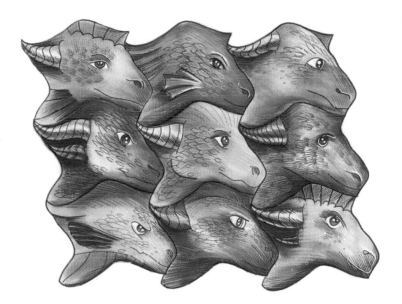

8 With value established, add tiny details like textures. To make things pop, use a white gel pen or a paint marker and add some highlights.

Artist Trick

Don't overcomplicate your tessellation subject; focus on overall basic shape and avoid tiny details or intricate edges.

FREE-FORM ART

Research Richard Gregory's café wall illusion. It is a series of staggered parallel lines with rows of black and white boxes that seem to move or shift. Try to re-create this psychological illusion.

CHAPTER THREE

Realistic Portraits and Figures

One of the key differences between a cartoonish and a realistic portrait or figure, aside from anatomical accuracy, is how you use line and value. If you start a person off with heavy black outlines, you're on a path to creating something stylized. To make a piece that's photolike, it's all about capturing how light travels across the curves of our bodies.

It's very easy to over-render. We immediately want to add facial features with thick, black lines, emphasizing the nose, eyelids, lips, and so on. It's just how most of us were taught to draw faces as kids. Let's try to unlearn this formula a little; instead of looking at the face in lines, imagine it instead more abstractly, like a landscape. You have areas that protrude from it like your brow, nose, chin, lips, cheeks, and eyelids. These catch light more and are often areas where you'll see highlights since they'll hold less shadow. Meanwhile, areas like the eye sockets, under the lips and nose, and the sides of the face are like indents or slopes that are angled inward, and they hold shadow.

PORTRAIT STATUE

 With a 2H or your lightest pencil, quickly sketch the head of the statue. Feel free to flip to step 8 to get a sense for the finished product.

Artist Trick

Use a series of horizontal and vertical lines to map out proper proportions.

 With light shading, indicate the darkest areas: around the eyes, ears, underside of hair, chin, and nostrils.

Darken them a bit. Blend out to the mid-tone area. Strokes should follow the form and shapes of the features you are defining.

 Define the eyes, face, nose, ears, and lips. Finish the planes of the face, from mid-tone to a light value. Leave blank areas that catch the light.

CONTINUED ▸

PORTRAIT STATUE CONTINUED

5 With an H, push the values in a select few areas like the upper lid and nostril—but don't use tons of pressure.

6 Think of the hair and eyebrows as solid shapes and not thousands of strands. Have your strokes follow the waves and curls of the hair, with breaks where highlights are.

KEY-DETAIL PRACTICE
For eyebrow hair, start with strong dark vertical strokes in the center of the face, then fan and angle them out to lighter, shorter strokes as they reach the edge of the face.

 Feel free to indicate some loose strands of hair that add definition.

 To create realism, shade the areas around the head with a mid-tone. Take one final look and see what areas could use a bit more pop.

PORTRAIT

 Create a very light sketch of the face with a 2H pencil. Draw the neck and some shoulder area.

 Lightly indicate the shadow planes on the portrait, and follow the direction of the facial structure.

Try smudging with a pencil in this one to blend together and out the light indication of shadow to create a smooth mid-tone. Shade following the contours of the face.

 Use an H and add the darker values around the inner eyes, under the nose, corners of the mouth and upper lips, ears, jawline, and neck. Smudge to blend into the mid-tone area.

CONTINUED ▶

 5 Add the value of the hair, neck, and shoulders.

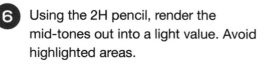

Artist Trick

For tiny details, smudge with a small tool like a cotton swab or tissue that's been tightly rolled into a point.

6 Using the 2H pencil, render the mid-tones out into a light value. Avoid highlighted areas.

TECHNIQUE STUDY

For tiny highlights like in the eyes, around the lips, and the nostrils, it is sometimes easier to use a white paint marker than to erase or shade around them for that highlight.

 Use darker strokes for eyebrows and hair. Push the darker value a bit under the neck, eyes, and nostrils, and where the hair is in shadow. Soften and blend out.

8 Instead of outlining the face, use a mid-tone/light value for the background, roughly stroke it in, and then smudge out. Keep the edges of the face crisp.

KEY-DETAIL PRACTICE
Notice how the white of the eye is really more of a mid-tone and is darker toward the upper lid. The pupil is more of a starburst than a circle and can disappear into the upper iris. Add highlights in the iris area and in the white of the eye.

FASHION FIGURE

 Start by lightly sketching the pose, almost like a literal stick figure, but indicate the angle of the hips and shoulders. Also pay attention to proportion and scale. Our figure is leaning against a handrail.

2 Lightly sketch the head and torso, then the limbs.

TECHNIQUE STUDY

Grab a magazine and, in your sketchpad, create a series of gesture drawings for the figures inside. Start out with a stick figure like the gesture tech study image and flesh out or ghost the overall shape of the figure.

Sketch the clothes; follow the folds with lines as they flow around the form.

 Lightly render the shadow throughout the form. We should just have two values right now: the paper and your light shading.

CONTINUED ▶

FASHION FIGURE

 5 Build up a darker mid-tone by following the shadows of the muscle structure. Indicate facial features just by their value.

KEY-DETAIL PRACTICE
Use value, not lines, to show muscle through subject shading; use light soft shading.

 6 Render the mid-tone and lighter values of the cloth. Blend the values of the cloth, then indicate folds with a darker, harder edge.

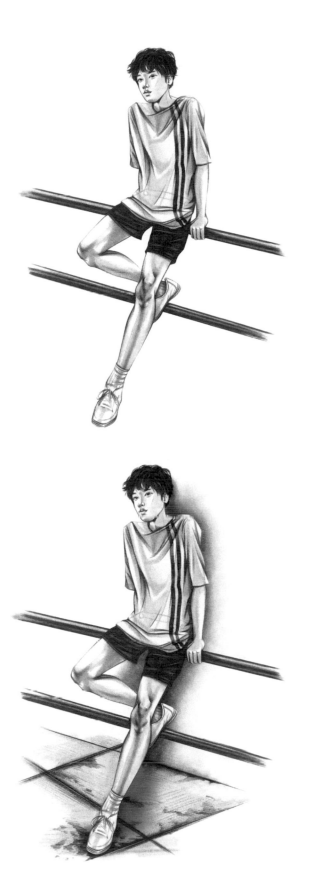

 7 Add darker values; for skin creases, use a soft line and blend out. Rough in facial features. Since the head is small, draw only what is visible. Draw in clothing pattern and details.

 8 Add a dark shadow beneath the figure to ground it and emphasize the light source. Lightly shade in the area around the figure to finish without a harsh outline.

WARM AND COOL PORTRAIT

 Lightly sketch the model's features with a 2H pencil.

 Use a neutral-colored pencil to just very lightly indicate the overall areas of the darkest shows.

 Focus on the cool side; pick a blue and lightly blend over the shadow, slowly changing up direction to get a cool base. Continue to blend beyond the shadow into the mid-tone with two or three other blues, like navy, eventually going lighter where the highlights are.

 Repeat step 3 for the warmer side with reds, pinks, and oranges.

CONTINUED ▸

 Blend together where the warm meets the cool to create a seamless transition. Use a third shade like a red-violet to do this.

 **KEY-DETAIL PRACTICE**
Blend the warm color into the cool. Start with orange on one side and blue on the other and begin to overlap. Switching back and forth between the two colors, add pressure and swirls to mix.

 The hair, some of the clothes, and parts of the face on the cool side are almost black, but blend darker shades of blue, purple, orange, or red to get a warm and saturated shadow.

 Add some details such as individual hairs, highlights of color like bright red reflecting off hair strands, and details in the clothes. Define some hard edges around the nose, jawline, and ear.

 Color in a background and add some highlights with a white paint marker.

FREE-FORM ART

Using only two colors, draw a graphic portrait where one color is the light and the other is the shadow.

CHAPTER FOUR

Fantastic Animals

Animals are my favorite subjects. There's such a variety of colors, patterns, and personality in them, and you never run out of subjects to tackle. I love drawing animals and plants with common characteristics such as a specific color or design they share.

The key to drawing a realistic animal is to have a good reference. I usually have two or three photos of the same animal in similar poses, and grab my favorite elements from each one to draw in my piece.

Now, to create a convincing creature based on fantasy, you need to base that creature's concept on something in reality. For mythical beasts, I look at multiple reference sources of different animals. For a dragon, I love using the head of a crocodile or snake, since their mouths are expressive and fierce; the body of a big cat like a lion, since they have great muscle structure; and the wings of a bat or a unique bird. If you're drawing from your imagination without a deep understanding of anatomy, most people would notice some kind of flaw in its structure and it'll be less believable.

So, let's tackle these next few exercises and approach them as we did our still lifes and figures. First, we'll start with a simple stick gesture of the overall body. Then, think of shapes for the creature's structure. After that, we will add values, then finally the details.

DAPPER DOG PORTRAIT

 Lightly sketch the head and shoulders of the dog. Indicate the placement of the eyes, nose, and mouth.

 Sketch out the animal's rough portrait. Draw the shapes of the eyes, nose, and mouth.

 The subject has fur, so you can be a little rough with your strokes. Using an H pencil, render out the area where the shadows and mid-tones lie.

 Render the darker area. Blend the mid-tones into the shadows for soft edges.

TECHNIQUE STUDY

Look at three different skin types of animals, such as scales, fur, and feathers. Render each type of texture in your sketchbook. Hair can be achieved by quick short strokes, features may be drawn as a mix of shape and value, and individual scales can be observed for how light interacts with them.

CONTINUED ▶

5 Finish by blending out mid-tones to light, leaving the paper visible where there's area of highlight or major light.

Artist Trick

Keep harder edges in areas like the skin wrinkles of the bulldog.

6 Detail the facial features and contrast with some darker values. Then add some individual hairs. For the dog's pattern, rough it in with some loose, broad pencil strokes.

 Rough in a value for the background. If things look too harsh, smudge them a little to soften the edge.

 Go back in with a white marker and add some life to the portrait with highlights. Areas around the nose and mouth are wet and often reflect light; same with the eyes.

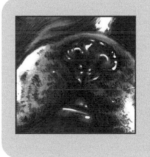

KEY-DETAIL PRACTICE

Focus on a wet area, such as the nose, and observe how light and shadow interact with it.

OCTOPUS

 Using a 2H or H, create a light sketch of the animal's structure with lines and shapes.

 Further define the animal's form and indicate any markings lightly, especially if they are a strong value.

 Lightly render the mid-tone and shadow areas. There's no fur and little texture, so you can smudge or blend it smooth if you'd like.

 Now, with a B pencil or more pressure, render out the deeper shadows. Be sure to softly blend the transition from mid-tones to shadows.

CONTINUED ▶

 With an H pencil, lightly render out the shift of mid-tones to a lighter value, leaving highlights and major lit areas alone.

6 Indicate a bit of a setting here—you don't just have to rough out a solid color. If your animal looks too subdued, pump the contrast a bit with some more areas of darks and lighter values. Sketch in a background to add more contrast.

 Finish the creature with important details like patterns and texture. Use a variety of strokes and marks for surfaces.

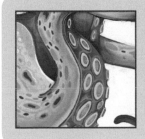

KEY-DETAIL PRACTICE
Focus on rendering the suction cups on the tentacles through value and not lines.

Add the final little touches that will bring life to the piece. Use a white marker for highlights, and define with dark strokes a hard edge or two.

FIERCE GRIFFIN

 Draw this mythical creature using your imagination, attaching multiple animal parts where you think they should go. Using line and shape, lightly sketch your creature's form.

Artist Trick

When choosing reference photos, make sure they all have the light source coming from the same direction.

 Define your sketch beyond simple shapes by including some anatomical structure. I like to start with the head and build downward.

TECHNIQUE STUDY

Traditionally, the Chimera had a lion's head, a goat's body, and a serpent's tail. It is more broadly defined as a creature made up of different animal features. Design your own chimeras in your sketchbook.

3 Lightly rough in the mid-tone and some shadow areas. Try smudging to soften the texture, if applicable, to your creature.

4 Define darker shadow areas and blend them into the mid-tones, then blend into lighter values.

CONTINUED ▶

FIERCE GRIFFIN CONTINUED

5 Render in facial elements, body texture, and using a light, soft stroke, add a bit of muscle structure in the arms, chest, and legs.

6 To ground your animal, add a shadow beneath it or scenery like a tree or rock. Use a variety of strokes and pressure for some abstract texture that indicates enough organic elements without having to draw each detail.

7 Detail things like fur or feather texture using short, defining strokes. Boost shadows for more dramatic lighting. Add details like pupils, claws, teeth, and horns.

KEY-DETAIL PRACTICE
Use varied strokes to create a setting. You can re-create grass with short dashes, sand with dots, and leaves on trees with rough scribbles of different value.

8 Add a mythical sword or figure to the scene to create a narrative.

COLORFUL DRAGON

 1 Imagine your dragon in a specific position, like laying down and guarding treasure. Using line and shape, sketch out its form.

 2 Define the form by lightly sketching the basic anatomy.

TECHNIQUE STUDY

Constantly refer back to references to see common points in anatomy to figure out how to sketch them. Most creatures have the same basic structure represented in slightly different ways. When attaching a head to a different body, use the neck and clavicle area as a meeting point. For wings, connect them near the shoulder and scapula. In merged areas, draw an anatomical structure that is a cross between the structures in both references.

 Using a neutral shadow color, lightly rough in areas covered by mid-tone and shadow.

4 Decide the body color for your dragon, and apply more pressure and change stroke direction to blend color and shadow together. Slowly build up value and blend neatly into mid-tone.

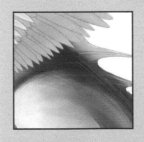

KEY-DETAIL PRACTICE

Toning down the saturation of a color can make the dragon more realistic. Practice blending complementary colors together or more neutral shades into more primary ones to see what works for your tools.

CONTINUED ▶

5 Blend the mid-tone into the lighter value, not touching areas in major light. Change your color to a lighter shade.

6 Indicate texture by using a variety of pressure, colors, and marks to represent scales, horns, feathers, ridges, and so on.

 Add more details; a slant to the eyelid or a hint of a smile can bring some personality into your dragon. Choose a couple of key areas to really push detail in the scales, wings, and claws.

8 Add your own background scene.

FREE-FORM ART

Draw a portrait of your own pet or favorite animal from a photo.

CHAPTER FIVE

Hyper-Detailed Drawings

In previous chapters, I often used the term *rough in* to indicate the hint of texture and detail through quick mark-making with selective strokes like dashes, lines, and dots. We also focused on details of the piece, like the face, and we left less important areas less rendered.

With hyper-details, the goal is to make a piece that is so realistic your viewer thinks it's a photograph. Instead of indicating details with rough marks, you look at each individual mark in your reference—its stroke, value, and shape—and you redraw it exactly. You're more conscious of hard and soft edges and how value is blended together. For smooth surfaces like a face, you need to softly blend shadow so well that you can't see the paper's texture or the strokes of your pencil. For hair or eyelashes, you'll start with a light blanket of value underneath; then draw each individual hair, applying various degrees of pressure; and gradually transition between lights and darks through hundreds of tiny strokes. You'll use a lot more fine lines than broad, thick strokes, especially with highlights, where you can use a small 0.4 mm-tipped white marker or a blade to scratch into the actual paper (this is more effective if you're working in ink). It can seem intimidating, but the end result is quite amazing.

CRAWLING 3D SPIDER

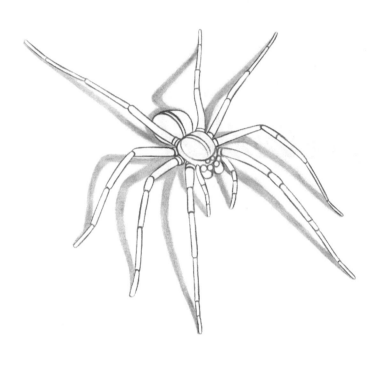

 With a 2H pencil, lightly sketch the spider's body and drop shadow to look like it's crawling.

 **KEY-DETAIL PRACTICE**
Try to add a drop shadow roughly to a spider sketch first; experiment with where the shadow transitions in value.

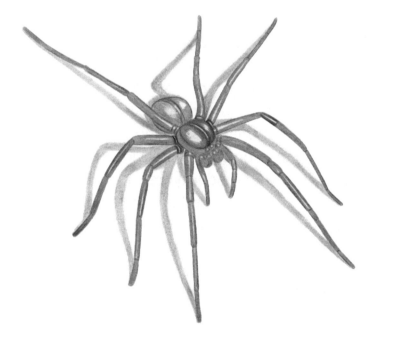

2 Lightly sketch the shape of the shadow and the highlights. The spider is mostly dark with long streaks of highlights on the legs and round highlights with some mid-tone on the body.

 In your mid-tone and shadow area, add some value with an H or classic B pencil, and blend smoothly with a smudging tool.

Artist Trick

A cotton swab might be too thick for this; try using a wad of tissue rolled up into a point.

4 Darken the mid-tone using a B or 2B, and blend out the harsh contrasting value of the body.

CONTINUED ▶

5 Finish the body and switch back to an H. Blend smooth from mid-tone to light, leaving the white highlights alone.

6 The pieces of the drop shadow touching the ground will have the darkest value, and will curve inward toward the body. Very lightly render the drop shadow shape and blend out.

7 Go in a bit darker now with the drop shadow, such as where the legs touch the paper. Smudge or blend out.

8 The spider's body is pretty close to the ground, so just slightly darken the shadow beneath him.

REALISTIC OWL

 Break down the owl into shapes: a long oval for the body, a curved teardrop for the wings, and a circle for the head. Lightly sketch out.

 Develop your sketch lightly, indicating features, and sketch out the shape of shadows and significant patterns on the wings.

 Lightly render in the mid-tone and shadow areas, and blend softly.

 Blend out mid-tone to light areas softly.

CONTINUED ▸

 5 This owl is dramatically lit, so finish by pumping up the shadows and blending cleanly.

Artist Trick

Notice that some areas have high contrast with shadow and light transitioning into each other quickly. Try just smudging here.

6 You'll notice individual thin lines of feathers, especially around the face. You can go in with a fine-line white marker or try scratching with a blade. Or, look at the darker strokes around the face and render those.

TECHNIQUE STUDY

To re-create layered feathers or hairs, work from light to dark, gradually building up value with pressure. Start with large strokes, then as you get darker, refine it to smaller, shorter ones. Finish with highlights.

 Render feathers in where you see a mid-tone value.

KEY-DETAIL PRACTICE
Re-create the feather pattern and texture. The feathers should be captured in value only; markings can be with more bolder lines.

 Finish by rendering out the darker details, especially on the patterns and details around the eyes. Add a background to give the owl a sense of place.

BEAUTIFULLY BOLD PERSON

 Flip to step 8 to see the finished product. Break down the image into simple shapes and lightly sketch it out.

 Now, lightly sketch more specific details, planning out the facial features, breaking down the outfit, and mapping out significant shadows.

 3 With an H pencil, lightly render the area covered by mid-tone and shadow, and blend smoothly, following the contours of the face and clothes.

 4 Smudge out or pencil-render the mid-tone to light area.

CONTINUED ▸

5 Now focus on hard edges and soft edges. You'll see hard edges more in the folds of clothes. Soft edges are more like the soft curves of your face. Start in the lighter areas and render the hard and soft edges.

6 Continue rendering out into the mid-tone and shadow area with the edges. You should end up with a drawing that is just value.

KEY-DETAIL PRACTICE
The values around the face are light and delicate. Using only value, render the tip of the nose and nostril area following the curves of light and shadow, no lines.

 Now refine details like the hair and costume features. Instead of just dropping down random lines to add texture, pay attention to each individual mark, note its value in the piece, and apply selective pressure to draw it.

Artist Trick

If you need to lighten an area but don't want to erase, try white chalk or charcoal.

 Finish by pumping the contrast, making the darkest areas almost black. Use a fine-line paint marker to hit highlights in the hair, in the eyes, on the skin, and in the accessories.

FOOD ART

1 With a pencil, lightly sketch out the shapes of the cake and its setting.

2 Refine the sketch to show the cake's structure and its toppings.

 This is a bright, colorful scene without deep dark shadows or cools. Use a warm brown and very lightly render significant dark areas.

4 Very lightly color and render out the larger blocks of color such as the frosting, the setting, and the cake layers.

CONTINUED ▶

 5 Apply more pressure to add more value to these areas. Analyze the shapes of the spongy pockets in the cake layers, or notice the smoothness of the fruit and candy. The edges touching the frosting are likely darker since they browned in the cake pan. Little details like these help you push the realism.

6 Individually draw each sprinkle and make them bold. Start with the lighter colors and gradually go to the darker, overlapping some.

TECHNIQUE STUDY

For bright rainbow color schemes, using a neutral or complementary color can kill the chroma and muddy up the colors. Try using a darker shade of a warmer color like burgundy, burnt sienna, or yellow ocher to add value in something so bright. In your sketchbook, blend these or similar shades into bright, saturated colors to try to make a value bar.

 7 With the color added, boost the contrast by making some of the darks darker.

8 Finish with highlights—there's a lot of reflective surfaces on the candy and fruit, and even the sprinkles and some cake capture the light. Hit those with your white fine-line marker.

KEY-DETAIL PRACTICE
Experiment with drawing sprinkles. Will you make tiny dots that take longer, or larger ones? Will you use full pressure or slight pressure? See what works best to re-create them.

FREE-FORM ART

Choose a subject and create a magnified drawing of a section. It can be the threads woven in cloth, the eye of a cat, or the leaf of a plant. Re-create every little detail.

About the Author

ANGELA RIZZA graduated from New York City's famed Fashion Institute of Technology in 2011 and has been creating artwork inspired by wildlife around her home and her favorite childhood stories ever since. She enjoys teaching art and creating activity books that help others learn to draw and use their imagination. She lives in Mahopac, New York.